A Different Kind of Christmas
Youth Study Edition

A DIFFERENT KIND OF CHRISTMAS: LIVING AND GIVING LIKE JESUS

An Advent Program by Mike Slaughter

Book: Christmas Is Not Your Birthday

In five short, engaging chapters, readers are inspired to approach Christmas differently and to be transformed in the process.
978-1-4267-2735-1

DVD With Leader Guide

Video programs about ten to fifteen minutes each to accompany and complement the book, one video for each of the five chapters. Leader guide contains everything a leader needs to organize and run a five-session Advent study based on the book and videos, including discussion questions, activities, and flexible session lengths and formats.
978-1-4267-5354-1

Devotional Book: Devotions for the Season

Five weeks of devotional readings for program participants. Each reading includes Scripture, a brief story or meditation, and a prayer.
978-1-4267-5360-2

Youth Study Edition

A five-session Advent study for youth in support of the program. Written in a style and approach to inspire youth. Includes leader helps.
978-1-4267-5361-9

Children's Leader Guide

Complete lesson plans for a five-session Advent study for younger and older children, including activities and handouts.
978-1-4267-5362-6

Mike Slaughter's

A DIFFERENT KIND OF CHRISTMAS

Youth Study Edition
by Kevin Alton

Abingdon Press
Nashville

Mike Slaughter's
A Different Kind of Christmas

Youth Study Edition
by Kevin Alton

Copyright © 2012 by Abingdon Press
All rights reserved.

This book is printed on acid-free, elemental chlorine-free paper.

ISBN 978-1-4267-5361-9

12 13 14 15 16 17 18 19 20—10 9 8 7 6 5 4 3 2 1

MANUFACTURED IN THE UNITED STATES OF AMERICA

Contents

Introduction

Something about Christmas has bothered me for a while. For a long time I didn't say much about it. In fact, I found that you can get through just about any family holiday a lot easier if you keep your opinions about anything to yourself: sports, politics, the actual holiday you are celebrating, whatever. Smile when a camera is pointed at you, and try not to be late. Success.

But when you have kids, all that changes. Suddenly the last thing anybody wants to hear is, "Yeah, we're not really doing Santa with our kids." We felt there were good reasons for it, such as being truthful and focusing on the true meaning of Christmas. But family and friends have questioned our decision, and no answer we've given has satisfied them.

So I was a bit surprised at a request I received from my mother-in-law last year: She wanted me to write her a Christmas story. Me? The guy who robbed your grandchildren of Santa? You want me to write a Christmas story?

It wasn't easy; I really wrestled with it. I knew I would be tripping over exposed nerves with any possible storyline, and I worried that all characters would be presumed to be family members. After a couple of over-vented first drafts, I came up with not only a storyline, but a vehicle for discovering what really bothers me about Christmas.

The story, called "Peace on Earth," is about Mabel, an older saint who through a shipping error arrives in heaven with all of her Christmas decorations. Jesus and an angel are dispatched to talk her out of keeping them, especially considering the imminent arrival of her husband the following week.

"I'm quite tired now," declared Mabel. "Christmas is exhausting."

Seeing an opportunity to redeem herself in the conversation, the angel took the lead. "What about Christmas exhausts you, Mabel?"

"Oh, it's not just any one thing, dear." Mabel pretended to clean her lens-less glasses. "It's everything—from putting up the decorations, to remembering who you're supposed to invite over, to sending cards you want to send and cards you have to send, to getting the just-right gifts for just the right people, it's just . . . everything."

The angel pressed on. "But a few minutes ago when you were talking about the 'spirit of Christmas' you didn't mention any of those things. You were talking about peace and goodwill." She paused for a moment, then added, "It just seems like all of that exhausting stuff would only distract you from enjoying peace and goodwill."

"Oh it does, dear," said Mabel. "That's why I decorate so. To remind me when I get home how much I love the peace and goodwill. I like to be reminded. It makes it all seem worthwhile again." Mabel's expression lit up with sudden recollection. "I forgot when you booted my Christmas village into next week that I was about to ask you both something—why doesn't anyone else decorate here?"

"We don't need decorations because we don't need to be reminded," Jesus said gently. "Peace and goodwill are all that anyone does here. It's not a time of year. It's not a thing you can forget. It's who we are. Here, the time you used to spend reminding yourself about peace and goodwill you just spend doing it."

I think my mother-in-law liked the story. I'm certain she thinks she's Mabel. (She's not.) I was surprised to find how much peace *I* found in the story, finally having words for my frustration: The way people want us to be at Christmas is how we should be *all the time*. Somehow we've reduced it to a single day.

It seems that I'm not alone. I was excited when I was asked to write this book, allowing me to join the conversation about rediscovering the meaning of Christmas.

The book is obviously not the first of its kind; in fact, Mike Slaughter's book *Christmas Is Not Your Birthday* is the basis of the churchwide study, *A Different Kind of Christmas,* of which this book is a part. My hope is that you will find my book useful, whether reading it by yourself or as a group, in drawing you closer to God during this Advent season.

Using This Book

Each chapter of this book mirrors a chapter from *Christmas Is Not Your Birthday* by Mike Slaughter. Drawing on Slaughter's challenging thoughts about Advent and Christmas, I have written ideas for youth to consider, including leader helps for those using the book in a group. These ideas are organized in sections, as described below.

You may want to look at the Slaughter book, but don't feel that you need to, as this book is written to stand on its own and can be used very effectively that way.

Reading and Reflecting

This section will lay out some of the main thoughts from Mike Slaughter's book, along with examples from my own family and ministry experiences. It concludes with a discussion of the main text for the chapter. If you're using this book as a devotional, think of this section along with the main Scripture as the first devotion.

Going Deeper

Here you'll find three additional devotions using Scriptures that complement the main text for the chapter. If you are using this book with a group, a helpful approach would be to have group members commit to completing the reading and devotions before coming together as a group.

Making It Personal

These are some reflection questions that look back over the devotions and are intended to be answered alone. If you've completed the devotions during the week, it might be helpful to review these questions right before you go to meet with your group. If you're not meeting with a group, you can use them whenever you like.

Sharing in Conversation

These group questions can serve as an icebreaker to open your group time together. They should also allow anyone who hasn't read the chapter to be drawn in to the conversation.

Bringing It to Life

Here you are given two fifteen-minute activities designed to engage your group with the material in a new way. (You can use one or both activities, depending on the needs of your group.) Supplies are minimal, but be sure that someone is in charge of bringing anything necessary to the experience. Most of the activities wrap up with one or two additional discussion questions or a peek back at the text.

Listening for God

Each chapter concludes with a prayer. You can use this prayer, substitute one of your own, or design a prayer activity that includes the group.

Blessings to you on your journey through Advent!

1. Expect a Miracle

1. Expect a Miracle

Therefore, the Lord himself will give you a sign: The virgin will be with child and will give birth to a son, and will call him Immanuel.

Isaiah 7:14

READING AND REFLECTING

The Ghost of Christmas Past

What makes Jesus really difficult to deal with is that he never has been what we think we want.

The early Jewish community of Jesus' disciples wanted a messiah who would overthrow the existing Roman rule, restoring Israel to its former power. It's safe to say that we've been perfecting that misunderstanding of Jesus ever since, always trying to bend him to our will instead of the other way around.

Mary very well may have been the last person to get Christmas just right. Of course, she did have the benefit of *not knowing* that it was Christmas. She was distracted by the direct revelation from an angel that she was to become pregnant and that the child would be called the Son of God. She would have been worried that she was unprepared and unqualified for such a task. She would have been bracing herself for how this coming Christ would affect her life—what would change, and what she would face as a result of simply being willing to participate. And in that moment, she was willing. She was open to this new vision for her life, no matter how difficult, no matter the cost. Does this sound like Christmas at your house?

Somewhere we've squeezed the meaning out of our Jesus, particularly at Christmas. An event that at its inception called for making deep personal sacrifices and using ordinary means to accomplish extraordinary things has come to sputter with empty meaning, like an old neon sign. We've lost the miracle once offered, and we don't seem moved to seek it out again. Christmas Day has become what it never was meant to be. One could argue, in fact, that it wasn't meant to be a day at all—that in living lives that reflect Christ in and through our relationships, there would be no need for a day of remembrance. But we love what we've made it.

Personally, I don't love it. In fact, sometimes I can't stand it. I miss the miracle. I want to *wonder* again at the unbelievable truth of the person of Christ. But I can't, because everyone keeps asking me what I want from the store as a gift, and what I think my wife or kids might want. It all makes me a little sick: the full-court press marketing blitz; the raging swell of debt for families that can't afford it; the complete sidestep by Christians of anything Christ-like as we tear down our barns to build bigger barns to store all of our self-imposed blessings.

I think what hurts the most is our misappropriation of the genuine goodwill that exists within the mayhem. I think people really are *trying* to do good in some fashion at Christmas; they're just doing it in a way dictated by consumer culture. Everybody should have something at Christmas, right? I've been on the receiving end of that kind of goodwill many times and have received it as a miracle in each instance. I'll never forget our elementary school janitor bringing my family a Christmas meal we couldn't afford. Or the time as a freshman in high school that a family "adopted" ours and showered us with gifts we wouldn't otherwise have received. Or the Christmas after my mom died, when my girlfriend's mother (now my mother-in-law) overspent to make my pile of presents equal in hugeness to her own two children's, knowing that at our house, in the first year of my mom's absence, we couldn't bring ourselves to celebrate with a tree and gifts.

Those are treasured, life-changing memories for me. But the shower of gifts veils the terrific example of how we should live in sacrificial relationship with each other *every day*. Every day we should find someone who can't afford dinner. Every day we should seek out a family in need of clothing. Every day we should extend love and acceptance to those around us who are hurting. The miracle of Jesus as we observe him at Christmas is that we didn't get to pick him out, and it's impossible to return him the next day if we decide he doesn't fit our lives. Jesus came to transform the *every day* of our lives.

I'm inviting you this year to hear with new ears the story of Christ's coming. Expect the miracle of Jesus. Prepare yourself to receive the change he brings to your life. Consider the cost. And rejoice with a clear vision as God begins a new work in you.

The Sign

Our Christian tradition owes a great debt to the Jewish faith and Scriptures. Without them, Jesus might have been interpreted as simply a renegade deity flung into the face of every world religion. Our Gospels show Jesus to be the fulfillment of Old Testament prophecies, and in so doing they intertwine our faith with a long and wise tradition. In Isaiah 7:14, we find this: "Therefore, the Lord himself will give you a sign: The virgin will be with child and will give birth to a son, and will call him Immanuel." If we look back at this exchange between God and Ahaz in Isaiah, then flip ahead to read Matthew (1:18-24) as he neatly puts a bow on the fulfillment of that Old Testament promise through the birth of Jesus, we might tend to forget what happened in between: hundreds of years passed. Generations came and went. Ahaz, in Isaiah 7, declined to ask God for a sign but was given one anyway. Surely he believed that the promise would be fulfilled within his lifetime, especially considering that the sign was given in response to an immediate military threat.

Small wonder that Jesus' disciples thought he had come to overthrow Rome. They'd been raised on centuries of tradition that their military woes would be addressed just as soon as the sign came. As Jesus walked and talked and taught and lived a life that existed only for love's sake, it had to sting a little that those closest to him had completely missed the point of his existence—those who called themselves his disciples and were the first Christians.

Can we really say at Christmas that we've understood the miracle of Jesus any better than they did?

GOING DEEPER

Are You Shy?

They say that fear is a powerful motivator, but so is poor self-image. We've all shied away from doing new things, perhaps important things, because we feel that we aren't good enough, smart enough, tall enough, or just because we might fail. Has this happened to you? When? What were the circumstances? Do you regret your decision?

Read Luke 1:46-48.

Do Mary's words sound like the words of a shy girl? Why or why not? When the angel first told Mary what was going to happen (Luke 1:26-38), was she a little more guarded in her response? What do you think had changed?

How can you find the kind of joyful expectation that Mary showed when God asks things of you in your own life?

Letting Go

Paul, one of the most celebrated apostles, experienced a remarkable journey of faith. He was a Roman citizen and a well-schooled religious figure; in short, he had it made in the culture to which he was born. As he began to follow in Jesus' footsteps, those achievements and accolades began to fall away. Paul was undeterred; he had found a new purpose in sharing the love of Christ.

Read Philippians 3:7-11.

Have you let Jesus change your life at this level? What are some things you have let go in order to follow Jesus more closely?

Do you miss those things? Were they all "bad" things, or have you found that even good things can become distractions in your relationship with God? What are some examples?

If Jesus doesn't figure this centrally in your life, what's holding you back? What are you afraid to let go of?

Surprised by God

Have you ever been surprised when something you did turned out all right? What makes us doubt ourselves so easily? Mary and Joseph had already experienced quite a journey by the time they brought Jesus to the temple and were no doubt well-versed in trusting God along the way. Even so, when Simeon met the young Jesus and praised God, they couldn't believe the words they were hearing.

Read Luke 2:25-33.

When was the last time you were just blown away by the movement of God? What were the circumstances?

Sometimes we encounter great things in good times, but often we find our faith renewed by God's actions only after we wrestle in the darkness for a while. What difficulties do you imagine that Mary and Joseph faced in raising Jesus to this point? How rewarding do you think their experience at the temple was?

It's possible that you are still waiting for your "temple moment." How do you find strength to press on through difficult times when following God?

Making It Personal

Spend a few minutes thinking back over the Christmases you've experienced in your life so far. What are some of your favorite memories? Why do they stand out?

What are some of the good things about gift giving and what generally is referred to as "the holiday spirit"?

How much Jesus is in your Christmas? It may sound funny to ask in that way, but it's an important question. If Jesus isn't the focus of your Christmas, what is? How do you feel about that?

What can you do this year to prepare yourself for the miracle of Jesus coming to us?

Are you prepared to make the necessary sacrifices in your life to welcome Jesus fully? Do you already know what some of those sacrifices will be?

Are you open to new visions from God for your future? Is it possible that you've already been stifling some glimpses of your future, because you're afraid of what it might mean for your life? Are you willing to let go of that fear and instead begin to trust?

SHARING IN CONVERSATION

Spend some time with a group discussing these questions:

1. What are everyone's plans for Christmas this year?
2. Can anyone share an experience in which they overcame their fears or self-doubt to do something for God?
3. What kinds of sacrifices can we make to follow Jesus more closely? Are there big, obvious things in our lives that need to go?
4. Has any one of you ever felt *led by God* to do something? What was it? What did that feel like? Did you follow through?
5. If Jesus were to ask you one question about your family's Christmas from last year, what do you think it would be?

Bringing It to Life

A Very Matey Christmas

Supplies: A child's (functioning) telescope

Spend a few minutes passing the telescope around your group, taking turns looking through it. What can group members see within the room that they might not have noticed before? Small objects, stains in fabric, even the texture of the walls might receive new attention. What do you see?

When everyone has had a turn, ask someone to write the text from Isaiah 7:14 on a sheet of paper. The words should be small but visible to the naked eye. Ask someone who hasn't seen the verse to read it through the telescope, with one restriction: They have to look through the wrong end.

Give everyone an opportunity to try the same thing, looking through the wrong end of the telescope. Was anyone able to read the verse?

It is possible to read the verse, but it's definitely more difficult. Spend a few minutes talking about the "lens" we look through when celebrating Santa Claus and the highly commercial nature of today's Christmas, instead of making Christmas a holiday celebrating Jesus' birth. How do Santa Claus and the practice of exchanging gifts confuse the message of a humble Jesus born to a family of meager means? Does that bother anyone? Why or why not?

A Sight for Sore Eyes

Supplies: An inexpensive set of magnification glasses (the stronger the better)

As in the previous activity, pass the magnification glasses around your group, taking turns trying to see through them. If people wear glasses already, they should remove them. Try reading from a book. If you're in someone's home, get some old photographs and place them on the floor, then stand and try to identify people in the pictures. Any luck? Any headaches?

As a final exercise, lay out a long string or a line of white tape from one end of the room to the other. Pick a volunteer to stand at one end, wearing the glasses. Spin the volunteer for a minute or so and then have them try to walk down the line. It should be fun to watch. You can come back at the end of your discussion time and let everyone try it who wants to.

Ask the initial volunteer: What did that feel like? We've all been a little dizzy, but how did it change things to have your eyes affected as well?

Let everyone discuss: In your own life, how did you choose the quality of your eyesight? Did you get to choose? If not, what determined your eyesight?

Have people in the group ever tried to deny problems with their eyesight— for example, holding off on getting glasses or contacts, pretending they could see farther down the eye chart, and so on? How did that go?

If we're uniquely equipped as we follow Christ, how similar or different should we expect our vision to be when compared with the vision of those around us?

What are some ways that we can embrace our own vision and encourage the vision for Christian living of our friends? What can we accomplish together?

LISTENING FOR GOD

God, help us this Christmas to rediscover the miracle of Jesus' example. Show us how to live our lives in a way that remains open to your leading and makes us part of your great work. Amen.

Thinking and Writing

Read the questions, then use the space below to write your thoughts.

What's the favorite Christmas present you ever gave, and why?

What is the closest thing to a miracle that you have experienced?

2. Giving Up on Perfect

2. Giving Up on Perfect

The angel said to her, "Do not be afraid, Mary, for you have found favor with God. And now, you will conceive in your womb and bear a son, and you will name him Jesus...." Mary said to the angel, "How can this be, since I am a virgin?"

Luke 1:30-31, 34 NRSV

READING AND REFLECTING

Return to Sender

Somewhere we started to get the idea that all of Christianity can be comfortably featured on a postcard: "Dear rest of the world—wish you were here." We want our churches clean and orderly with everyone dressed just so, with families that get along and dogs that don't bark too much. Where the heck did that idea come from?

Extended to Christmas, things get confusing fast. American Christians particularly seem to have a roasting-fire, gather-the-family, all-is-well mental postcard that they're trying to achieve each December. Santa is usually on that postcard, leaving us the gifts we wanted, because we deserve them. And while there's usually at least a moment within those madcap days around December 25th when everybody sighs and murmurs, "Ah, now *this* is what Christmas is all about," mostly we find ourselves crashing from one disappointment or over-scheduled event to the next. Someone is late. Something didn't arrive in time. You don't like my casserole. I had to sit by creepy uncle Irwin again. It's just not...*perfect,* like we imagined.

The problem with all of this is that no one ever promised you *perfect.* I know, I know; I grew up thinking I'd heard the promise too. But it was just clever advertising. We share a collective memory that never existed, pulled together from things we care about. One thing that's certain is that *Christmas* never promised perfection. Christmas was a home-wrecker from the beginning. As we see it in Scripture, Christmas hijacked the lives of a young couple with no notice and very little discussion. Mary and Joseph: God is coming to earth; we need a place to start. You're it. Sorry about the mess.

I spent a few years trying to strip away all of the extra that we've tagged onto "the real meaning of Christmas." I wanted to cast off all of the cards, presents, carols, and other odds and ends that were cluttering what I was certain must be the *genuine meaning* somewhere at the center of it all. But it was like peeling an onion: eventually I realized that my quest for a perfect Christmas was all layers with nothing at the center. All tears and stink. Did I not go *back* far enough?

Eventually I realized that I was still looking for that perfect postcard image, just one with Jesus on it instead of Santa. But guess what? That postcard doesn't exist either. If you go back far enough through all of the years and ways that the church has observed Christmas (including rejecting it a time or two) you eventually come upon a pretty sizable gap between the birth of Jesus and the first time anybody decided to celebrate it again. You'll also come upon a startling piece of trivia: not only is Christmas not *your* birthday, it's not really even Jesus' birthday. There are a handful of traditions and beliefs about how that day came to be associated with *Jesus'* birth, but none of them hold that he was actually born on December 25th, a calendar date that wouldn't have existed yet anyway. So...well, shoot.

I didn't know what to do. I had all this pent-up distaste and disgust with how we had ruined the *real meaning of Christmas* and couldn't we please just get back to *that*, only to find that there was no *that*. Or was there? What did

Christmas really offer us before we made it into the several thousand things that we wanted it to be?

Presence, not presents.

Jesus' birth was a sign. Immanuel: God with us. And sure, he would one day crawl, then stand, and eventually walk and begin to show us the way, but in the moment of his birth—this first instance of what we call Christmas—he was simply *here*. We are loved, even if things aren't going our way. If we are stuck in darkness, he comes to that darkness with us. Not a postcard image, but somehow...

It's perfect.

Girl, Interrupted

Girls, imagine you're getting ready for your wedding day. (Back with you in a minute, boys.) Invitations have been sent, relatives are making travel arrangements, happy feelings spill out of every pore. *Anything* unexpected at this stage would be unthinkable. There's too much in motion. But then a bomb drops.

I'm going to be pregnant?

Whatever the circumstances leading to that pregnancy, chaos is certain to break loose in your life. People will talk. Some will be angry. Some will be supportive. Consequences will line up at the door. Why now? Not *now*!

Yet that is precisely where we find Mary in Luke 1:30-31 (NRSV): "The angel said to her, 'Do not be afraid, Mary, for you have found favor with God. And now, you will conceive in your womb and bear a son, and you will name him Jesus.'" Afraid? What about angry? But anger and fear didn't seem to be her response in verse 34: "Mary said to the angel, 'How can this be, since I am a virgin?'" She accepted the news at face value, questioning only the apparent physical impossibility of pregnancy. According to Scripture, Mary had not yet had a sexual relationship with a man.

Disaster. But Mary rose to the occasion. Much is made of Mary's youth, but at the time there was no adolescent marinating period between childhood and adulthood. As a girl preparing for marriage, she was clearly prepared to begin her adult journey. We see no evidence of a woe-is-me attitude, no "I deserved better than this." She was resolute. These are my circumstances; this is my God. I can only move forward in trust. She worked it out, with God's help and support, and eventually with Joseph's help and support too. (Welcome back, boys.)

GOING DEEPER

A Hard Truth

We have put so many pretty bows on our faith over the years that it's easy to forget something very simple: We were never promised an easy road. We are meant to follow Jesus' example. That sounds nice, but it gets a little complicated when we realize that Jesus, while living a life of sacrificial love toward others, managed to make some people so mad that they eventually killed him. It's easy to forget that while our lives as Christians are pretty comfortable and persecution-free these days, it wasn't always that way, and still isn't in many places around the world.

Read 2 Corinthians 11:24-27.

Does Paul's experience sound awesome? Paul may be bragging about his suffering to make a point, but the suffering is real. Have you ever had to suffer for your faith in some way?

Do you think of suffering as "part of the deal" or as something that you don't deserve? Why?

Does looking at the lives of Mary and of Paul give you some resolve for facing hard times, or make you want to avoid them even more?

Here With You

Most of us don't like to be alone. Even if we do like it for a time, we like feeling that somewhere out there, someone cares about us and wants us around. Sometimes that feeling is found in the comfort of leadership, such as knowing (even if we hide it) that our mom or dad is in charge. When our leaders change, we find it unsettling. A new pastor, a new youth worker, even a substitute teacher at school can shake us.

Jesus' disciples were no different. They had spent three years with Jesus and were disturbed to realize that he would be leaving them. Read John 16:5-7.

What did Jesus promise would happen when he went away?

Read the passage again. What did Jesus *not* promise? Are we guaranteed good times and everything that we want?

What does the presence of God guarantee you in your life?

You've Got a Friend

When nearly any life situation arises, our mind almost instantly asks, "Who can I talk to about this?" Sometimes the list of people is long, but sometimes it's very, very short. No doubt you've experienced things about which you wondered if there was *anyone* you could confide in. Do you have a "go-to" friend you can talk to about anything? If so, have you told them lately that you appreciate them? You should.

Read Luke 1:36.

Why would the fact that Elizabeth was also pregnant make Mary feel better about her own pregnancy?

When you're facing a difficult time, do you tend to seek out people who are in or have been in the same circumstances? If so, why? If not, what do you do?

Have you ever had the opportunity to offer that kind of help to someone else? Did you offer it?

MAKING IT PERSONAL

Have you ever gotten bad news around Christmastime? Think back to that incident. What was the news? How did you receive it? How did it affect those around you? How was your experience of Christmas affected that year?

What do you think of as the "heart" of your Christmas experience?

Think about the difference between being loved by God and getting the things that you want from God. Are those two things different in your life, or do they tend to be the same?

Can you think of a time in your life where the *presence of God* was all that you needed?

How have you been the presence of God to someone else? Can you think of a time when someone else was the presence of God for you? What was that like?

How can you find God's presence a little more this year at Christmas?

SHARING IN CONVERSATION

Spend some time with a group discussing these questions:

1. What is the biggest Christmas disaster that you can remember? Did things work out at the end?
2. What kinds of things do you think of when you hear the words *perfect Christmas*?
3. If you were Mary, how would you have taken the news from the angel? Who would you have told first?
4. What do you think Mary would have to say about the way we celebrate Christmas today? Why?
5. Why *don't* we like mess and disorder in our Christmases? Why do you think we want things to be perfect all the time?

Bringing It to Life

You're Unbelievable

Sit with your group in a circle. Go around and have each person say one wildly untrue thing about something they did or experienced in the past—the more ridiculous, the better. ("When I was in third grade, I invented a rocket that runs on recycled dreams. I still have it; I use it to get rid of nightmares, and I ride it to get the mail.") When everyone has done it, go around again and tell another story. This one should be a little less crazy, maybe even including a little truth. The object of the game is to catch someone telling the truth, so eventually someone should tell a story that is completely true but *sounds* made up. If someone in the group catches on that the story is true, they should yell, "Truth!"

If they're wrong, the person who yelled is out and the round continues. If they're right, they win. You can play again at the end if you have time.

When you've stopped, consider this question as a group: Have you ever found out something that you believed but knew other people wouldn't? What was it? What did you do?

Talk about Mary's response to the angel's news. Did her response seem reasonable? Understated? How would you have responded?

Sketchy Christmas

Supplies: 3x5 note cards (or small scraps of paper); pens, pencils, or markers

Distribute to everyone in the group a piece of paper and something to write with. Then ask everyone to spend a few moments thinking of a single item that they would include in a picture of a "perfect Christmas." The item can be whatever comes to mind—a tree, a fire, Jesus, a dog. When all group members have thought of an item, ask them to draw it on their paper and put the picture in the middle of the group on the floor. When the drawings are in the middle, work together to arrange them into a scene. Try to make all the group members as happy as possible about where their part of the scene ends up.

When your scene is finished, talk about it. Is it what anyone would call a "perfect Christmas"? Why or why not?

Now that the group's Christmas scene is finished, is anything missing? If so, what? If the group decides that something super-critical is missing, someone can quickly draw it and add it to the scene.

Now, as a group, begin to remove one thing at time from the scene, beginning with the least important item. What goes away first? What ends up being last? How do you decide what is and is not important at Christmas?

LISTENING FOR GOD

God, we're sorry for the mess we've made of Christmas and for not accepting it as the beautiful mess that it already is. Help us to find your presence this year at Christmas, to be content with that, and to follow you by doing those things for which we are uniquely gifted. Amen.

Thinking and Writing

Read the questions, then use the space below to write your thoughts.

Was the first Christmas "perfect"? List some of the things about it that were not perfect.

What's your idea of a perfect Christmas? Is there such a thing?

3. Scandalous Love

3. Scandalous Love

Then the LORD said to me, "Go and love your wife again, even though she commits adultery with another lover. This will illustrate that the LORD still loves Israel, even though the people have turned to other gods and love to worship them."

Hosea 3:1 NLT

READING AND REFLECTING

Loved

Too often we've let our impossible search for perfection carry over to how we view ourselves, demanding perfection there as well. Natural insecurities in our human relationships as we grow up can evolve into similar feelings toward God—how could God possibly love *me*? I'm clearly from the trial-and-error pile. I'm not good-looking enough to invite people to church. The only things I'm good at aren't "church things." I'm useless.

That kind of thinking really causes problems when our feelings of inferiority seem to be confirmed through experience. Trying to fit in to a small group at church and feeling pushed to the side, volunteering for something and getting passed over by the leader—we create and believe our own lies about our insignificance.

Youth ministries (and parents, and schools) spend a lot of time trying to convince you that it's all in your head—that you are good enough, pretty enough, smart enough, whatever. And that's all true. But let's take it a step further. Let's say you're right—that you are lacking in looks, talent, and accomplishments. That wouldn't change one beautiful, overlooked truth: *Even if you are right about all of that, God loves you.* The makeup of your being is no mystery to God. All those Scriptures about us being loved by God include God's full knowledge of who we are. There is no cosmic "Oh . . . you."

God loves you, no matter who you are, what you've done, or what you haven't done. Period.

Bearing Fruit

I've been involved in youth ministry for a long time. For many years I was a volunteer in a local church. Eventually that became my full-time employment. Over the past few years my role in youth ministry has expanded to include training and encouraging other youth workers as well as a bit of writing. I love what I do.

When I was still in high school, I can remember my dad sitting down with me and my brothers around the kitchen table. My older brother was about to go off to college, and I could sense a heart-to-heart talk coming. We had all grown up in the church and knew all the answers to all of the questions you could throw at us about faith and Bible stories. But my dad trumped it all and told us that, while he knew we could always bring home the trophy for Bible Trivia, he didn't see the fruit of a relationship with God in our lives. We were all words and no action. I started to object, but I knew he was right. It was hard to make sense of at first, because we *did* do so much church stuff. What more could there be?

All of that knowledge is great. I wouldn't trade my knowledge of Scripture for anything. But I wasn't letting it change my life. I'd drifted from the relationship I'd experienced. We are called to more.

That conversation awakened in me a call to youth ministry. My early years working with youth were pretty hard; time and time again, I'd find myself turning away or trying to do things my own way. But when things got tough, I remembered what my father told us that day: A life transformed by God bears fruit.

Where is the fruit of your relationship with God? Have you turned away from the God who loves you, even when you do?

A Day in the Life

This might be the weirdest story you've ever heard from Scripture. Brace yourself.

Hosea was a prophet of God. Being a prophet in those days was no easy slice of pie. Generally you ended up doing unexpected things with your life so that God could make a point to people who hadn't been paying attention. Sometimes you had to tell them that the end was near. Sometimes you had to promise destruction. In Hosea's case, he had to marry a prostitute.

God wanted to show the nation of Israel how they had made God feel in their relationship. God was steadfast; ever true. Israel had been sleeping around a bit, so to speak. They'd gone against their promises of faithfulness to God and instead were doing whatever they wanted. So God told Hosea to take the prostitute named Gomer (salt in the wound, if you ask me) and marry her. And have children. And give those children names that meant things such as "not-loved" and "not my people." Yikes.

Gomer was a career-minded girl, and soon she was spending more time at work than she was at home. Point made, right? We get it, God. You tried to be the "good husband" to us and we were unfaithful.

Not quite. Read Hosea 3:1.

If you're reading most versions of the Bible, I encourage you to go ask your pastor what sacred raisin cakes are. Beyond that, note the movement of God in the living analogy that Hosea's life had become: The faithful lover goes after the one who has run from the relationship. God, who loves us in spite of all we know and despise about ourselves, goes one further and doesn't even wait for us to come back or straighten up or even realize that we're in the wrong. God comes after us.

GOING DEEPER

The Habit of Missing the Point

On any given day, we're pretty adept at ignoring encounters with God that can occur through the people around us.

Most of us have routines. As we move through our day, the best way to engage us is to interrupt those routines. When that happens, of course, we don't like it: Why are you interrupting my routine? So the needs and joys of the people in the margins of our lives go ignored—the kid no one talks to in the lunchroom, the person who delivers our mail, the gas station attendant, the checkout clerk at the grocery store. Mom once told us not to talk to strangers, but somewhere along the line we decided it meant that everyone outside our routine should remain a stranger—even people that we encounter every day.

Jesus points out the fault in that kind of thinking in his parable of the sheep and the goats. Read Matthew 25:31-45.

Who are the people on the fringes of your life? Can you name them? Why don't we engage those people? What are we afraid of?

Fully Known

When we have a friend we really trust—with anything—then being in their presence is like wrapping up in a warm blanket. There is such a sense of security in that relationship. We feel that we no longer have to pretend; we can just be ourselves, because that person already knows everything about us. Often we don't even have to talk to them to feel that sense of security. Just being around them is enough. They know us, and they still love us. That's enough for just about anybody in a friendship.

We forget sometimes that God knows us this fully as well. Read Psalm 139:13-18.

Why do you think we feel such safety around friends who know us, but sometimes we feel intimidated by God's intimate knowledge of us? Is any of it guilt? How well do you really know God?

Obviously we're not capable of fully understanding the mystery of God, but are there areas where you've missed opportunities to know God better?

Birds of a Feather

Mary receives most of the pregnancy attention in the gospels, which is probably fair considering that she was carrying Jesus. But if you're just examining circumstances, Mary and Elizabeth actually have a lot in common. Mary gets most of the credit for taking on the challenge of an unexpected pregnancy, but Elizabeth's pregnancy was unexpected too. Elizabeth was advanced in years; she had no reason to anticipate having a baby and likely had made peace long ago with the idea that she wouldn't have children. The realization that she was going to have a baby could easily have been just as unsettling for her as the news was for Mary. There were fewer consequences, to be sure, for Elizabeth; but just as unsettling.

Yet Elizabeth exhibited only joy at the news and offered companionship to her cousin Mary. Read Luke 1:39-45. What do you think the support from Elizabeth meant to Mary?

Have you ever used a challenge in your own life as an opportunity to help someone with a similar challenge? If you have, share it, as you feel comfortable.

MAKING IT PERSONAL

Are there things in your life that you've always felt you do "for God" that you're now beginning to realize don't actually help the relationship? If there are, share some examples.

In what ways do you practice the presence of God, not just at Christmas but all year long?

Compared with other times in your life, do you feel closer to God now or farther away? What happened to make that change in your relationship?

Our lives affect the lives of those around us. Can you think of specific ways you try to use the circumstances of your life to bring the people around you closer to God? Have people ever used circumstances in their lives to help you? If so, share some examples.

SHARING IN CONVERSATION

Spend some time with a group discussing these questions:

1. What do you love about Christmas? Where do you feel the most love from others at Christmastime? Where and how do you feel you best show love toward others?
2. Is there anything about Christmas that has become less meaningful to you over the years, such as presents you have to give or people you have to see? Are there other things about it that bother you or have less meaning?
3. Where do you feel like you are most *known* at Christmas? Where are you most comfortable?
4. Do you feel that your group does a good job of simply being with people in your community who might not experience God's love otherwise? What are some ways the group is currently doing this? What are some new ways it could do this in the future?

BRINGING IT TO LIFE

Unlovable

This activity requires a little honesty and could get a little personal. Know your group and be sensitive about pressuring anyone to talk who doesn't want to. Begin by saying that no one *has* to share and that anything shared will be kept confidential within the group. Nothing leaves the room. Also, you should-n't need to say so, but any laughter or poking fun during this exercise will prob-ably be counterproductive.

Ask everyone to think of times in their life when they felt least lovable. They may have been sick, depressed, recently broken up, or just have been in the middle of a bad time. When everyone has a time like that in mind, ask the group to think of an instance in one of their least lovable times when some-one showed them love. Go around your group and ask anyone who is willing to share to do so.

What kinds of things did your group have in common in unlovable times? Were there any similarities between how you were shown love in those instances?

Spend a few moments thinking about Mary. How might she have felt unlov-able as we see her in Luke 1? Who showed her love? How?

Being Love

Supplies: A piece of paper and a writing utensil

One major part of our commitment to following Christ is to *be* the love of Christ to those around us—not just to those with whom we have day-to-day relationships, but to everybody. It's hard to do, but it's part of our job. As a wor-shiping body in a local church, this call multiplies exponentially. With more of us working, we're suddenly capable of doing so much more in our com-munities and around the world. This love can look like a thousand different things! Spend a few minutes compiling ways that your group has been involved in lov-ing others outside of your group and your church. Include in your list activi-ties or events that your group no longer carries out.

Which things on your list are your favorites?

Are there any activities on the list that have been discontinued that you miss? Why did they stop?

Are there any new things that you should consider adding to your list? What opportunities can you think of to create new ways of loving your community?

If your group is willing, work together to create one new way to be the love of Christ to those around you. Or, if you prefer, revisit some of the things from your list that have been discontinued and choose one to bring back.

What will the group need to do to make this happen? Who do you need to involve?

LISTENING FOR GOD

God, in Jesus you've given us such a beautiful example of how to live a life of scandalous, selfless love for others. Help us to find that love in our own lives, both as a group and individually. Help us to live our lives in such a way that when others see us, they also see you. Amen

Thinking and Writing

Read the questions, then use the space below to write your thoughts.

Think of a time when a friend let you down. How did it feel, and how did you respond?

Jesus spent time with people who had terrible flaws. Why do you think he did it?

4. Jesus' Wish List

4. Jesus' Wish List

"*The King will reply, 'I tell you the truth, whatever you did for one of the least of these brothers of mine, you did for me.'*"

Matthew 25:40

READING AND REFLECTING

Thinking Outside the Gift Box

What do you get for somebody who has everything? Choosing Christmas gifts is one of the most torturous social exercises known to humankind. It's our own fault that it has become that way; we've so numbed ourselves to simple gratitude that we make people jump through hoops just to give us something. What if the gift I buy is too big? What if they spend more on their gift for me than I do on my gift for them? And the granddaddy question of gift-giving: What if they don't like it?

Here's the answer. It was a gift. You cross them off your list of people that you give gifts to and warn your friends about their lack of gratitude. Oh, wait. We don't do that. We try harder the next year, probably even worrying more about it.

There almost aren't words for how far from the "spirit of Christmas" our gift giving and getting have brought us. For example, there wasn't ever supposed to *be* a "spirit of Christmas." It was just supposed to be the new way to live. But instead, we've sold ourselves a lie at Christmas. It was easy to do, too; we like the lie. It makes Christmas about us.

To unpack the lie at Christmas, we're forced to use our own Christmas terminology to see if we can sift some meaning out of the holiday. Which leads to an unusual question: What would Jesus want for Christmas? Not baby Jesus; this-year, present day Jesus. It seems a shame to leave him off the gift list.

My wife Britta and I have a delightfully imperfect history of gift giving— occasionally forgetting, sometimes overdoing, at times simply agreeing to let a holiday pass ungifted. I remember once when we were dating, I arrived to pick her up for a Valentine's date. I was invited in; I gave her flowers and sat down. She went back to her room and produced a wrapped gift and a card for me. I opened the gift, which was a CD I already had in my collection (a detail I kept to myself). I read the card. Hugs. And then she asked: "Where is my present?" I had no present. Tears. A long discussion followed, ending with a list of holidays at which we, as a couple, should expect to give and receive a gift and a card from each other.

It gets better. Three months later, in May, my birthday came and went with no card or present from Britta. In fact, there was no "happy birthday" or any other acknowledgment that I had aged. I was puzzled, but I let it slide. I waited nearly two months, and finally in mid-July I asked, "Hey, umm, it's no big deal, really, but, umm ... did you forget my birthday?"

Tears again. She hadn't forgotten it. She wasn't sure what to get me, and then as my birthday got closer she realized she didn't have any money, and she was embarrassed not to have a gift after making such a big deal of things at Valentine's Day. So she did the only sensible thing: stand very still and hope that I forgot my own birthday.

It was never about the gifts. Britta just wanted to know that she was special to me, highlighted by a little extra care a few times a year. And I just wanted to know that she loved me. We could have made it about the gifts; we could have decided how many and what kind and how much to spend. But somewhere in there, we probably would have forgotten that love started the whole thing.

Which is what we all do, to some degree, at Christmas. When we give Christmas gifts to people, do we intend for those gifts to show our love or Christ's love? Sometimes we can do both, but I think when most of us give gifts, we get the majority of the credit. How can we give ourselves back to God at Christmas?

Finding Jesus

The parables of Jesus provide fascinating insights into the mind of Jesus. In them we walk through his deeper motivations in ministry, digging in to what really mattered to Jesus. In Matthew 25:31-46, a passage we looked at in the previous chapter, Jesus got to the heart of how we are to live in service to each other. In this parable, Jesus welcomed a group into his kingdom, thanking them for all the times they fed him, clothed him, cared for him when he was sick, and visited him while he was in prison. The group was grateful but confused. "When did we do those things?" they asked. Jesus pointed out that anytime they did those things for people in need, it was as though they were doing the things for him.

Then Jesus turned and rejected another group, because they did not come to his aid to feed him, clothe him, care for him, or visit him in prison. Equally surprised, the group asked when they had ignored Jesus on each of those occasions. Jesus' answer still cuts deeply: Anytime we do not do those things for someone in need, it is as though we have not done them for Jesus. Ouch.

Don't sink into a deep depression about all the times throughout the year that you've left Jesus hungry, without clothing, sick, or unvisited. Just look ahead to this coming Christmas. You'll find loads of opportunities all around you. There are hungry people, people in need of shelter and clothing, people who are sick and in prison.

Find new ways to reach out to Jesus. It's all he wants for Christmas.

GOING DEEPER

Garden Math

I am always disappointed at the number of fresh tomatoes in our garden. Our watermelon crop is equally unsatisfying. I've just gone out to check on the bell pepper plants; again, to no avail. In defense of the garden, I haven't *planted anything*.

It sounds silly, but isn't that what we sometimes do? We continually expect a return with little or no investment in life. We want a good grade on a test for which we didn't study. We think people should like us no matter how badly we treat them.

Our spiritual gardens need planting as well. How can we expect to become more like Jesus without ever acting like him? Read 2 Corinthians 9:6-11.

What kind of "fruit" do you expect from your relationship with God? What kind of planting have you done to produce that fruit? Are there things that you do to improve your Christian witness, or have you been hoping that growth will take place by itself?

Self-fulfilling

The Gospels, particularly Matthew, show Jesus as the fulfillment of Scripture. Have you ever thought what it would feel like to *be* the fulfillment of Scripture? What if one day you realized that you were the embodiment of an ancient promise? Would you embrace it or run from it? Jesus embraced it. In fact, he stood up in the temple, read a passage from Isaiah, and then said, "Yeah . . . that was about me." Bold.

But guess what: we're supposed to be like Jesus. Read the passage he read from Isaiah 61:1-2.

Are you like that? I'm not saying that you're Jesus or God or anything. But as a regular human being, can you and I approach this kind of action in our lives?

If you were to *begin* to be like this, what would your first steps be? Who would you help first? Who would you comfort first?

Will you?

The Main Thing

Do you know why there's Daylight Savings Time? Do you know why you have to put certain food items in the refrigerator only after you've opened them? If you attend a church, do you know why the Sunday morning services are scheduled when they are? There are lots of things in life that we do simply because *that's the way we've always done them.* But when you don't know why you are doing things, the meaning behind what you do is sometimes lost.

Read John 13:34-35. According to these verses, what is it that Jesus says will show others that we are his disciples? What do most people think of when they hear the word *Christian*? What discrepancy do you notice between your two answers?

What about your life says *disciple* or *Christian* to those around you? Is it love, or something else?

MAKING IT PERSONAL

From my perspective, Christianity has gotten needlessly complicated. If "loving those in need" doesn't sum up your Christian experience, what kinds of things have you added?

Look again at Matthew 25:31-46. In what ways have you fed, clothed, and visited Jesus? In what ways have you missed those opportunities?

Have you been willing to make sacrifices for the benefit of others in need? Name some examples that you feel comfortable sharing.

Have you seen others making similar sacrifices for you or your family and friends? Again, name examples.

Can you think of new ways that you can begin to give back to those in need, particularly at Christmas?

How can you carry those actions beyond Christmas?

SHARING IN CONVERSATION

Spend some time with a group discussing these questions:

1. Who in your home is in charge of getting everyone's Christmas requests? Who is in charge of making sure that your relatives get gifts and that the Christmas cards are sent out?
2. Has your family ever tried to figure out a way to give something to Jesus at Christmas? What ideas have you discussed, or could you discuss?
3. After reading this chapter, are there things that you do or your family does at Christmas that you now see as "giving to Jesus"? What are some examples?
4. What ideas do you have for finding new ways that you, your family, or your church family can show love to those in need?

BRINGING IT TO LIFE

Feeding Frenzy

Supplies: Markers; several retail flyers from local department stores

Pass around the flyers and give everyone a chance, using the markers, to circle things they would want if price were not a factor and if there were an endless supply of money to use this Christmas. If possible, ask everyone to use a different color marker so that when they're done, you can tell who wanted what. If two people must use the same color, maybe they can use a different shape so you can still tell them apart.

When all the flyers have been marked, ask:

What did you feel like while we were doing that? Was it exciting? depressing?

When you were young, how did you tell your parents what you wanted for Christmas? Was it similar to what we just did, or did you do something different?

If you have brothers or sisters, did you ever fight about what you wanted? Did you fight about what you *received*?

If you could sum up your family's attitude and way of approaching Christmas in one word, what would it be?

Do you feel like your celebration of Christmas pleases God? Why or why not?

I've Literally Wanted This Forever

Supplies: Paper and writing utensils

Go around the group and ask each person to write down some of the gifts they received for their last few birthdays. If people feel comfortable sharing the information, have them read their lists out loud. Ask: Do you think anything you received might have been a little over the top? Were you disappointed with anything you received?

What do you think Jesus would have wanted for his birthday? (Even if we're not certain of the date, *he* probably knew.) Ask group members to turn their lists over and write one or two things that Jesus might have wanted for his birthday. Really try to put yourself in his time. Again, when people are finished, read the lists out loud. Is there anything surprising on the list? Is there anything funny?

How would you describe the differences, besides cost and technology, between what's on your own list and what's on your Jesus list? How has the idea of "want" developed since Jesus' time?

Look back at Matthew 25:40, 45.

What *hasn't* changed about what Jesus wanted since that time? Have we changed in what we offer to God? If so, how?

LISTENING FOR GOD

God, in so many ways we've exchanged your simple wish list for our own complicated wish list. Help us to see where we've made Christmas about us instead of about you. Teach us how, when we ignore those in need around us, we are ignoring you as well. Help us once again to find you in the least of these, and to realize that we, too, are the least of these. Amen.

Thinking and Writing

Read the questions, then use the space below to write your thoughts.

Mike Slaughter talks about Jesus' wish list. What are some Christmas presents that you personally could give to Jesus?

Think of one person you could help at Christmas, and how.

5. By a Different Road

5. By a Different Road

And they bowed down and worshiped him. Then they opened their treasures and presented him with gifts of gold and of incense and of myrrh. And having been warned in a dream not to go back to Herod, they returned to their country by another route.

Matthew 2:11-12 NIV

READING AND REFLECTING

Learning the Language

Christmas, as we've made it, no longer carries the message of God's love for people in need. If that's how we as Christians intend to leave it, then it's probably time to close up shop. It's one thing to stop caring about "the least of these"; it's quite another to make a mockery of the process in doing so.

At this point, it's probably too late to go back the way we came. Christmas no longer fits in the box we're carrying, so maybe it's time to find a new box.

Our Christmas is all about us; the coming Christ child is all about everyone else. Our Christmas emphasizes a warm, familiar story; Jesus emphasizes a hard look at how we've been living our lives for ourselves and how we can change to be more open to others. Our Christmas says, "It just wouldn't be Christmas without...."; while Jesus reminds us that no one should ever be without.

We've got to peel back the layers we've added, not to get to the center but simply to *get rid of the layers*. We're in a time of year when people are taking stock of things and gearing up to make New Year's resolutions. Think about the kinds of things people usually give up or commit to: less spending, less eating, more exercise, and on and on. Does that sound anything like the existence we're called to as disciples of Jesus—capping off a year's worth of overeating and self-indulgence with a year-end selfishness supernova before "getting back to the basics" of not gorging ourselves to death and joining a gym in January?

I don't remember what year it was that my wife and I decided we weren't going to do Santa Claus for our two boys, Grey and Penner. It seems like Grey was probably three going on four, and Penner would have been too young to care. We knew it would be an uphill battle with a lot of people, family included. In case you're unaware of it, people get really uptight when you take away one of society's sacred cows, especially if it's one where for some reason we've decided it's okay to lie to children. I remember my wife, Britta, saying at one point, "You know, I think it would be easier if we just told people we were converting to Judaism."

My argument for doing away with Santa was pretty simple. Setting aside all the consumer greed and corporate manipulation for a moment, I was concerned that when our boys became old enough to realize we'd made up the nice man nobody ever sees who brings them gifts at Christmas, they might also start wondering if we'd made up the God nobody ever sees who supposedly loves them. Or worse, that they'd project their ideas about Santa onto God, making *God* the invisible give-me-machine.

Britta has developed a better and less cynical approach. (It's a superpower she has.) She's the children's director at the same church where I work, and she regularly bites her tongue to keep from accidentally throwing Santa under the bus in front of our church kids. Britta had been trying to figure out how to deal with the issue of Santa Claus at church when she heard a story that she found helpful. It seems that some parents had brought their family to America, and they were wondering if they should speak English at home and teach their native tongue to their kids as a second language. They received some great advice: At home, speak only in your native tongue, because your kids will hear English everywhere else.

Perfect. Applied to the children at church, it means that during Christmas our leaders only talk about Jesus. The kids will get Santa everywhere else—even at home, for most of them.

Can you imagine a Christmas that was just about Jesus? *That* would be a different road, a real Christmas miracle.

Spoiler Alert

You know the scene in movies where somebody we know is a bad guy finds out something he shouldn't from someone in the movie who *doesn't* know he's a bad guy? Believe it or not, there's a scene like that in the Christmas story.

Magi, or wise men, were following a star that had appeared in the east, certain that it was a heavenly indication of a new king. Along their way, they stopped and asked King Herod if he knew where the infant king might be found. Of course, kings don't like competition. Herod played it cool and after a few questions asked the Magi to go find the child. He added one request: that when they found Jesus, they come back and tell Herod where he was, *so that Herod could worship him too.* At this point in the story, we all throw popcorn at the screen and yell, "Don't tell him!" Well, they *don't* tell him.

Read Matthew 2:11-12.

Bear in mind that the system of roads back then was not like it is today; there was probably significant effort involved in going back a different way. And while the wise men spared the life of Jesus and possibly their own lives by not going back to Herod, the Gospel of Matthew records a horrific mass-murder, at King Herod's direction, of all male children under the age of two. The first few Christmases were hardly a celebration. Joseph and Mary fled to Egypt with Jesus, where they remained until after the death of Herod.

Behind the glitter and spectacle of our modern-day celebration, we begin to glimpse some of the gravity of Christmas. These events were life-changing then and should be life-changing now. How has Christmas changed your life?

GOING DEEPER

Less Is More

We've talked about how God uses our gifts to work in the lives of others; an interesting flip side of that coin is that sometimes physical possessions limit our ability to take part in God's work. We can become so busy owning and maintaining *stuff* that we can't see beyond the end of our pile to the people living in need all around us.

Read Mark 10:17-22.

In the Scripture, Jesus set up the rich young man, giving him a couple of slow pitches to swing at. When Jesus finally brought the heat, the young man walked away, grieving.

In what parts of your life do you feel you're already doing a good job? In what parts do you hang your head? What parts are you hanging onto that might make Jesus say, "Yeah, but what about this?"

The rich young man walked away. Are you willing to make changes and keep going with Jesus? Why or why not?

Walking While You Talk

Different denominations (Methodist, Baptist, Presbyterian) exist largely because of disagreements over how we should believe—that is, the way we think about God, grace, and salvation. What often gets left aside in those disagreements is *how we should live*, which, for many of us, is more central to our lives.

Living. Doing. Being.

Read 1 John 2:28-29.

According to this Scripture, what's the best way to follow the example of Jesus? What does verse 29 say that will tell others we have come from God?

In your conversations at school about faith, do you and your friends focus more on what you should believe or how you should live? Why?

At the end of the day, does a person in need benefit more from what you tell them about God or what you *show* them about God through your actions? Why?

More Is Less

Does your family own a storage unit? Do you have a junk drawer or junk closet (or junk room)? Why? If someone stole something from it, would you even notice? Have you ever cleared everything out of it? How did that feel?

For all of the *getting* we do at Christmas every year, we do very little *getting rid of.* What happens when we run out of room? Seriously—what do you do when you run out of room?

Read Luke 12:16-21.

What parallels can you draw between the rich man's abundance and our current state of consumption?

Is there a point at which you could see yourself saying, "Enough!"? Are you at that point already? If not, what might it take for you to get there?

What could the rich man have done instead of tearing down his barns?

As we approach Christmas this year, do you find yourself satisfied with what you have, or are you also ready to tear down your barns to make room for more?

MAKING IT PERSONAL

Is there room in your life for the work of God's kingdom? Why or why not?

In what ways have you already participated in God's work? Did you do it alone, with your family, at church, on a mission trip?

How did that experience make you feel? Do you like the idea of doing it only sometimes, or would you like to work it into your life even more? Why?

Do the people around you know more about what you believe or how you live? How are the two related? Can an extreme of one or the other throw things out of balance? How?

We all have too much of something. As you've been reading, have you thought of places in your life where you need to thin out a little? What are they? Are you ready to take actual steps to do that? Why or why not?

SHARING IN CONVERSATION

Spend some time with a group discussing these questions:

1. How much of what you know about the beginning of Jesus' life is reflected in the way you celebrate Christmas?
2. Do you agree that Christmas has become something very different than the act of acknowledging and welcoming Jesus to our world?
3. What do you think Christmas might look like today if we threw it all out and started over?
4. What challenges would you face if you *really* wanted to reinvent Christmas in your home? in your church? in your school?
5. Your friends probably are aware that you call yourself a Christian. What is your life telling others about what is important in following Jesus?

BRINGING IT TO LIFE

I'll Know It When I See It

In this exercise, your group will work together to define what a certain inward belief "looks like" in the actions of the person who believes it. For example, a person who holds the belief "My house is on fire" will likely manifest that belief in the action of calling the fire department; checking the house for family and pets; quickly gathering anything that can't be replaced; or stopping, dropping, and rolling.

For each of the beliefs listed below, what actions can you imagine?

"I believe the milk in the refrigerator is past its expiration date."

"I believe it is time to get up and go to school."

"I believe the pan on the stove is still hot."

"I believe you're trying to steal my date for the prom."

When you've finished describing actions for all the beliefs, go back and add this kind of statement for each of them: "If I believed this, I would never _____."

Now repeat the entire exercise based on one final statement:

"I believe that Jesus came at Christmas to show us how to change our lives, so that we will live only to show God's love."

Look at the actions you came up with and compare them with the ways you celebrate Christmas.

Cutting Back

We're mostly thinking and talking about Christmas, but there is excess and waste in nearly every aspect of our lives. This is not exactly a pick-me-up thought, but it's true. All that waste and excess occurs naturally through inattention, neglect, or sometimes good old-fashioned intentional greed. But we're called to live so that we weed out that stuff, or else we'll be condemned to keep doing it. Our excess will become the center of our lives, and we'll become useless to the movement of God in our world. Let's think of ways to cut back so this won't happen.

We'll begin with Christmas:
• Where is the excess in our practice of Christmas?
• Is that excess within our control? Why or why not?
• If we could begin to remove some of the excess, where would we start?

Now let's look at ourselves:
• Where is the excess in our day-to-day lives? Is it in our possessions? in the way we spend our time?

- Can we immediately identify some things we need to change or get rid of? What are they?
- Have we already decided to cut some of that out of our lives? Why or why not?

How about our church group?
- How often does our group meet?
- Does each meeting serve a specific function, or do some of the meetings exist just because we've always met?
- Could any of our time be used more productively for God?

LISTENING FOR GOD

At last, God, we offer our gratitude for your intervention and forgiveness in our lives. Help us to see the ways we have wandered and to find our way back to the path, that our voices might more clearly lead others toward you. Amen.

Thinking and Writing

Read the questions, then use the space below to write your thoughts.

Has this book changed your feelings about Christmas? How, and why?

Imagine yourself as a parent. What would you teach your children about celebrating Christmas?

Organizing a Churchwide Program

A Different Kind of Christmas: Living and Giving Like Jesus is a practical and inspirational study for the Advent season. Based on Mike Slaughter's popular book *Christmas Is Not Your Birthday,* this five-week program will empower your family and your church to reclaim the broader meaning of Jesus' birth and to experience a Christmas season with more peace and joy than any toy or gadget could ever bring.

A churchwide Advent program for all ages will help people come to a deeper understanding of what the Christmas story teaches us about Jesus Christ and about God's will for our lives. It will offer opportunities for learning, for intergenerational activities, and for reaching out to the community.

RESOURCES FOR THE CHURCHWIDE PROGRAM

Adults
  Christmas Is Not Your Birthday—Book
  A Different Kind of Christmas: DVD With Leader Guide—Videos
  A Different Kind of Christmas: A Season of Devotions—Devotional
  book

Youth
A Different Kind of Christmas: Youth Study Edition

Children
A Different Kind of Christmas: Children's Leader Guide

Schedule Suggestions

Many churches have weeknight programs that include an evening meal, an intergenerational gathering time, and classes for children, youth, and adults. The following schedule illustrates one way to organize a weeknight program.

- 5:30 p.m.: Gather for a meal.
- 6:00 p.m.: Have an intergenerational gathering that introduces the subject and primary Scriptures for that evening's session. This time may include presentations, skits, music, and opening or closing prayers.
- 6:15 p.m.–8:45 p.m.: Gather in classes for children, youth, and adults.

You may choose to position this study as a Sunday school program. This approach would be similar to the weeknight schedule except with a shorter class time (which is common for Sunday morning programs). The following schedule takes into account a shorter class time, which is the norm for Sunday morning programs.

- 10 minutes: Have an intergenerational gathering that is similar to the one described above.
- 45 minutes: Gather in classes for children, youth, and adults.

Choose a schedule that works best for your congregations and its existing Christian education programs.

ACTIVITY SUGGESTIONS

Birthday Party for Jesus

An all-church party would be a good kick-off or wrap-up event. Take the opportunity to collect items as gifts for a local organization. Items for young children would be especially appropriate. Possible ideas include: children's books for a hospital library, baby supplies for a shelter, or school supplies for an elementary school.

All-church Food Drive

Lesson 1 in the Children's Leader Guide has instructions for families to organize a food drive and invite the entire church to participate. The food drive would last all five weeks of the study.

Service Projects

In Lesson 4 of the Children's Leader Guide, children will brainstorm ideas for a class service project. This idea could be expanded to become a church-wide service project. Alternatively, each age group could plan a service project and invite the whole church to participate.

Mike Slaughter is Lead Pastor of Ginghamsburg United Methodist Church in Tipp City, Ohio. In December 2004, Mike first challenged the people of Ginghamsburg to spend less on their families at Christmas and give an equal amount to what they spend on themselves to the Sudan Project. Through their annual Christmas Miracle Offering, Ginghamsburg has raised over $5 million for humanitarian relief in Darfur, Sudan. Mike has been named one of the top fifty most influential Christians in America, and has authored numerous books, including *Change the World* and *Upside Living in a Downside Economy.*

Kevin Alton is a youth worker, writer, musician, husband, father, and friend. He lives and works near Chattanooga, Tennessee, and is a regular contributor to youth resources, including YouthWorker Movement and his own Wesleyan resource for curriculum and community, Youthworker Circuit (www.youthworkercircuit.com).

Made in the USA
Lexington, KY
13 November 2012